The Sakki-Sakki Tarot Coloring Book

by Monicka Clio Sakki

Inspired by The Sakki-Sakki Tarot
for the Artist in Each of Us

ISBN 978-965-90681-6-6

Sakki-Sakki and logo and all related characters and elements are trademarks of Sakki-Sakki ©2016. MPress and logo are trademarks of MPress ©2016. All rights reserved. The artwork, illustrations, design, and contents are protected by copyright law. No part of this book may be reproduced in any form, including internet usage, without permission in writing from the author.

www.sakki-sakki.com
monickacliosakki.com

For a deeper dive into the meanings and interpretations of The Sakki-Sakki Tarot check out the companion book "Playing with Symbols".

SHARE YOUR COLORING:
#sakkisakkitarot
#sakkisakkicoloring

A black pen line is always the beginning.

At this point I don't care that there is no color yet, as I focus on form, first. When this part is done and the composition is in place, I start gathering my colors, one by one, till I have the whole pallete. It is only then that the match-making choices begin.

A crisp coloring page feels naked and lonely without color. This is where I invite you to step in! Get your colorin' on and color away, YOUR way.

You are The Artist.

With Love

Monicka Clio Sakki

SHARE YOUR COLORING:
#sakkisakkitarot
#sakkisakkicoloring

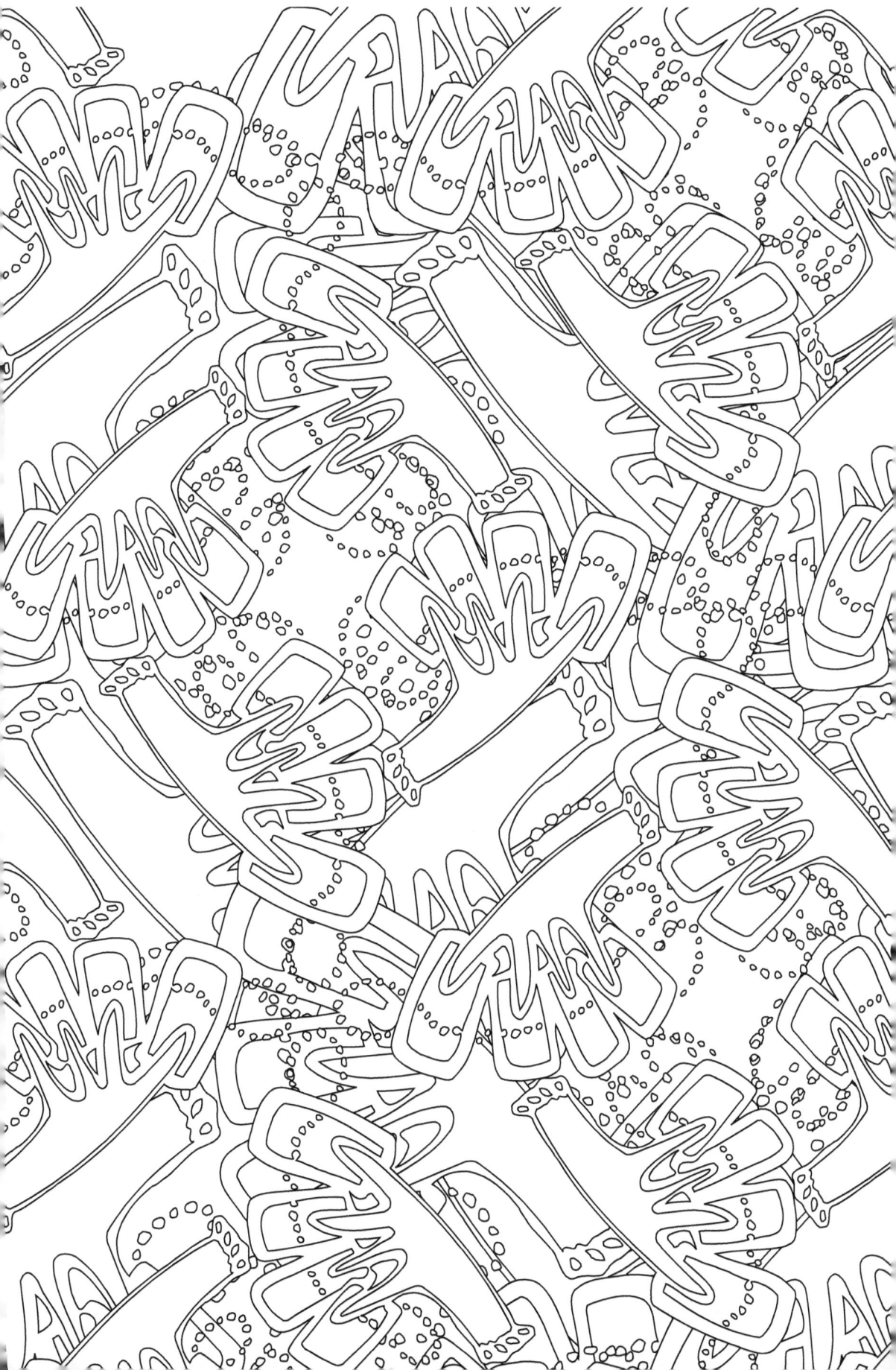

YOUR ARTIST'S STATEMENT

State your intentions. Your pencil has power!

THE SAKKI-SAKKI TAROT MAJORS

The Artist
Chiron

EVERYONE IS AN ARTIST
CRAFTING ONE'S LIFE • LIVING ONE'S TRUTH
ARTIST AS A PROCESS, NOT A STATE
BELIEVING WITHOUT KNOWING

0. The Fool
Uranus, Aleph

BLANK SLATE • NO MIND • NEW BEGINNINGS
EMBRACING THE UNKNOWN • INNER TRUST
NAIVETE • LEAP OF FAITH

I. The Magician
Mercury, Beit

CREATIVE INITIATIVE • MULTIPLE TALENTS
WILLPOWER • EGO • MASTERY • SYNTHESIS
CONCENTRATION • MAGNETISM • TRICKSTER

II. The High Priestess
Moon, Gimel

SPIRITUAL SOUL • INTUITION • INNER MYSTERIES
FEMININE WISDOM • SECRET KNOWLEDGE

III. The Empress
Venus, Daled

MOTHER OF ALL • CREATIVITY • FEMININITY
FERTILITY • ABUNDANCE • MOTHER NATURE

IV. The Emperor
Aries, Hay

Father of all • Leadership • Structure • Laws
Control • Frame-work • Authority • Ambition

V. The Hierophant
Taurus, Vav

GUIDE TO THE SPIRITUAL PATH • RITUAL
TRADITION • ORGANIZATION • EDUCATION

VI. The Lovers
Gemini, Zain

Relationships • Togetherness • Choice
The Great Union • Communication
Responsibility

VII. The Chariot
Cancer, Het

DETERMINATION • CONFIDENCE • BREAKTHROUGH
CONTROLING OPPOSITES • INNER STUGGLE
COMBINING THOUGHTS AND EMOTIONS

VIII. Strength
Leo, Tet

INNER CONFIDENCE • ENERGY • WILD HEART
STAYING POWER • COURAGE • SERENITY

IX. The Hermit
Virgo, Yod

SOLITUDE • INNER SEARCH • SELF DISCOVERY
REFLECTION • MEDITATION • SOUL NOURISHING

X. The Wheel of Fortune
Jupiter, Kaf

CHANGES • UNEXPECTED EVENTS • FATE
KARMIC UNFOLDMENTS • CYCLE OF LIFE

XI. Justice
Libra, Lamed

Countability • Balance • Justice • Karma
Cause and effect • Fair dealings • Legal issues

XII. The Hanged Man
Neptune, Mem

WAITING • SUSPENSION • NEWPOINT OF VIEW
CHANGE OF ATTITUDE • ENLIGHTENMENT

XIII. Death
Scorpio, Noun

PROFOUND CHANGE • TRANSFORMATION
DEATH & REBIRTH • END & RELEASE
DRAMATIC RENEWAL

XIII. One More Death
Scorpio, Noun

CREATE YOUR OWN CHANGE

XIV. Temperance
Sagittarius, Samach

BALANCED MIXING • MODERATION • HARMONY
EXACT COMBINATION • EFFORTLESS MASTERY

XV. The Devil
Capricorn, Ayin

TEMPTATION • INDULGENCE • MATERIALISM
CHAOS • RAW AMBITION • SECRET DESIRES
INTERNAL DARKNESS

XVI. The Tower
Mars, Peih

UNEXPECTED CHAOS • SUDDEN UPHEAVAL
VOLATILE ENERGY SEEKING RELEASE • RUIN AND
BUILDING OF A NEW ORDER • RECONSTRUCTION

XVII. The Star
Aquarius, Tsadik

HOPE • WISHES • THE BEAUTIFUL SELF
ONE'S UNIQUENESS • INSPIRATION

XVIII. The Moon
Pisces, Kouf

DREAMS • UNCONSCIOUS • INNER SELF
CONFUSION • DECEPTION • MYSTERY

XIX. The Sun
Sun, Reish

ENERGY • LIGHT • CLARITY • OPTIMISM
SELF AWARENESS • SUCCESS

XX. The Angel
Pluto, Shin

Awakening • Renewal • Realization
Revelation • Improvement • Self-celebration

XXI. The World
Saturn, Taph

COMPLETION • FULL CIRCLE • MANIFESTATION
SATISFACTION • SELF REALIZATION

THE SAKKI-SAKKI TAROT COURT

SUIT OF RODS

Intuition • Action • Energy • Vision
Courage • Creativity • Will • Inspiration
Transformation • Speed • Impulsiveness

Page of Rods

EAGER • RESTLESS • INTUITIVE
SINGLE-MINDED • ENTHUSIASTIC • MEANS WELL

Knight of Rods

Charming • Reckless • Curius • Un-stuck
Departure • Change of residence

Queen of Rods

HONORABLE • GENEROUS • LOVING • ENERGETIC
DIRECT • REALISTIC • SPARKLING PERSONALITY

King of Rods

MATURE LEADER • INITIATOR • ACTIVE • WISE
HONEST • DEVOTED • CHARISMATIC

SUIT OF CUPS

Feeling • Emotions • Unconscious • Mystery
Contemplation • Compassion • Moods
Sensitivity • Depth • Inner experiences

Page of Cups

IMAGINATIVE • THOUGHTFUL • SENSITIVE
LOVING HELPFUL • REFLECTIVE • DREAMY

Knight of Cups

APPEALING • ROMANTIC • NON-COMMITTING
EMOTIONAL AWAKENING • ATTRACTION
PROPOSAL

Queen of Cups

Deep • Sensitive • Creative • Caring
Compassionate • Mysterious • Visionary
Adorable • Practical • Achieving

King of Cups

Controlling powerful emotions
Generous • Responsible • Considerate
Reliable • Kind • Artistic • Professional

SUIT OF SWORDS

Thinking • Spirit • Mind • Reason
Dispassion • Opinion • Breath • Truth
Inspiration • Decision-making • Meaning

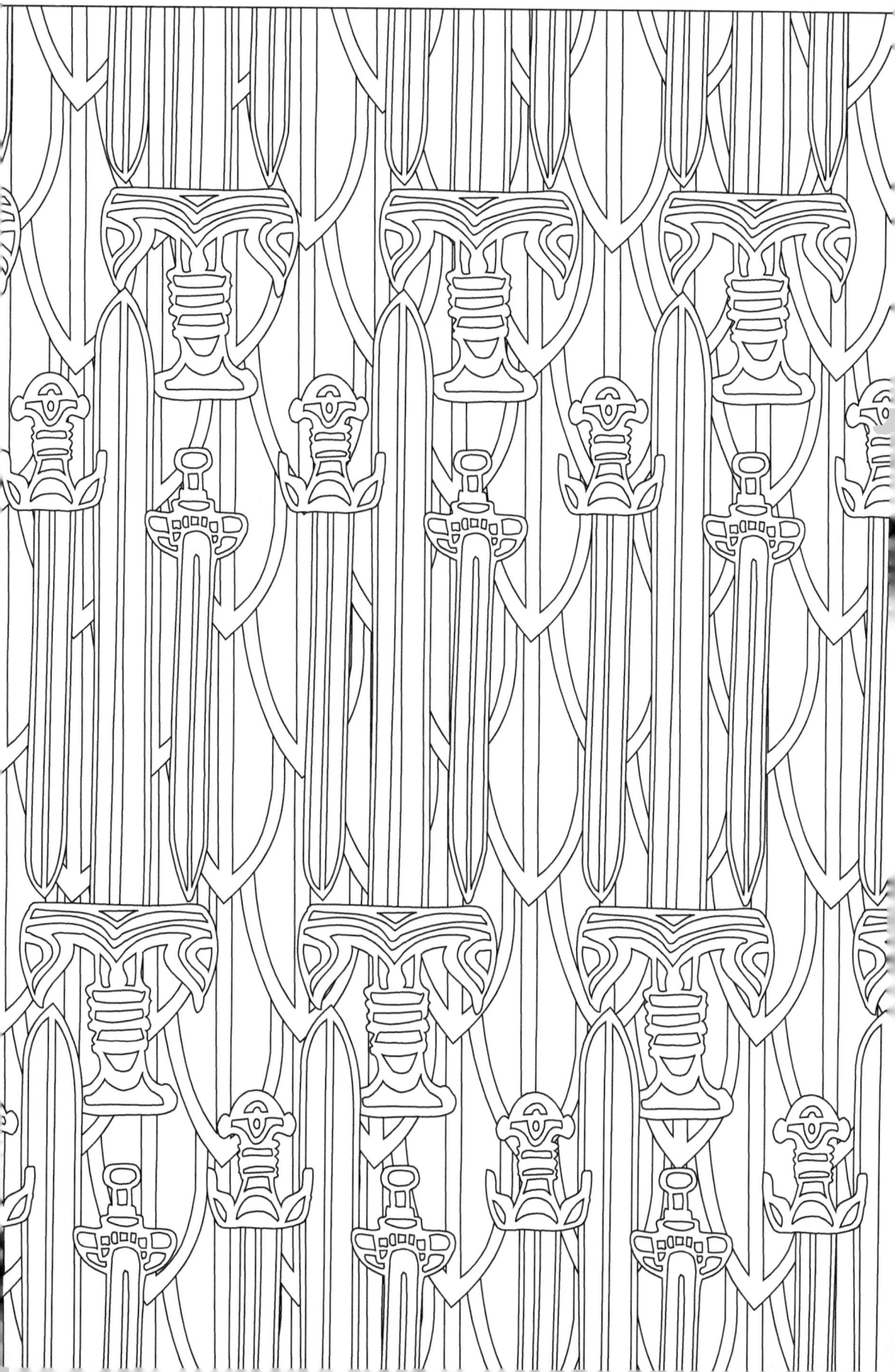

Page of Swords

INSIGHTFUL • RESTLESS • ALERT • VERSATILE
CURIOUS • QUICK MINDED • WELL INFORMED
DISCREET • CHARMING INSIDE AND OUTSIDE

Knight of Swords

BRAVE • FEARLESS • SKILLFUL • CAPABLE
HEROIC • SELF-ASSURED BUT INEXPERIENCED
IMPETUOUS • RUSHING

Queen of Swords

Wise • Intellectual • Independent
Serious • Courageous
Learning through painful experiences

King of Swords

SHARP-MINDED RULER • RIGID • DETERMINED
CONTROLLING • SUPERIOR • PROFICIENT
ANALYTICAL • FIRM • ARGUMENTATIVE

SUIT OF COINS

Sensation • Material World • Service • Work
Grounding • Practicality • Natural Cycles

Knight of Coins

Reliable • Methodical
Organized • Persistent
Waiting for the right moment to launch
a material project

Page of Coins

Scholar • Concentrated • practical
Bearer of news about monetary issues
Learning and planing on financial ventures

Queen of Coins

GENEROUS • PRACTICAL • WEALTHY • SENSUAL
LUXURIOUS • GOOD HEARTED • DIGNIFIED
NOBLE • LIBERAL • COMFORTING

King of Coins

STABLE • GROUNDED • WISE
SUCCESSFUL BUSINESSMAN
ABLE TO ACQUIRE WEALTH
COMBINES BUSINESS AND PLEASURE

CREATED WITH LOVE
FOR THE ARTIST IN YOU

Share your coloring:
#sakkisakkitarot
#sakkisakkicoloring

www.ingramcontent.com/pod-product-compliance
Lightning Source LLC
LaVergne TN
LVHW081355060426
835510LV00013B/1829